FEARSOME FORCES

WRITTEN BY MIKE CLARK

owerKiDS
press

Published in 2018 by
The Rosen Publishing Group, Inc.
29 East 21st Street, New York, NY 10010

Cataloging-in-Publication Data
Names: Clark, Mike.
Title: Fearsome forces / Mike Clark.
Description: New York : PowerKids Press, 2018. | Series: Strange
  science and explosive experiments | Includes index.
Identifiers: ISBN 9781538323625 (pbk.) | ISBN 9781538322666
  (library bound) | ISBN 9781538323632 (6 pack)
Subjects: LCSH: Force and energy--Experiments--Juvenile literature.
Classification: LCC QC73.4 C53 2018 | DDC 531.113--dc23

Written by: Mike Clark
Edited by: Charlie Ogden
Designed by: Matt Rumbelow

Photo credits: Abbreviations: l-left, r-right, b-bottom, t-top, c-center, m-middle. All images courtesy
of Shutterstock. With thanks to 2 – Sergey Nivens. 4: tl – Boule; tr – tsuneomp; bl – Jaywarren79;
br – Pat_Hastings. 5 – NikoNomad. 6 – lzf. 7: tr – xtock; br – Vadim Sadovski. 8: bl – Kues. 9: t –
photka; ml – Africa Studio; mc – Sashkin; mr – irin-k; bg – Sundra. 10: YanLev. 11: bg – KostanPROFF;
bl – Picsfive; tr – 34641646. 12 – Sailorr. 13 – hxdyl. 14 – Evgeny Karandaev. 15 bango. 17: bg – Sergey
Nivens; tl – Sashkin. 18: tr – Markovka; m – Ljupco Smokovski; b – Iakov Kalinin. 19 – Vit Kovalcik.
21 – sondem. 22 – imagedb.com. 23: bg – capitanoseye; tl – Garsya. 24: bl – mangax; br – Solomin
Andrey. 26: tr – Kyselova Inna; br – Georgios Kollidas. 27 – Nicku. 29: bg – Everett Historical; tr –
Rosa Jay.

Manufactured in China
CPSIA Compliance Information: Batch BW18PK: For Further Information contact
Rosen Publishing, New York, New York at 1-800-237-9932.

CONTENTS

Words that appear like this can be found in the glossary on page 31.

Force Firsts

A force is something that pushes or pulls an object. Forces often change the speed at which an object is moving or the direction it is moving in.

There are lots of different forces, and together, they make the **universe** work in the way it does. The four main forces that affect us every day are gravity, air resistance, friction, and magnetism.

GRAVITY

AIR RESISTANCE

FRICTION

MAGNETISM

Friction and air resistance are contact forces. This means that two things have to touch each other before these forces can take effect. Gravity and magnetism, however, are called action-at-a-distance forces. This is because objects do not need to touch other objects to be affected by these forces.

Without these four forces, the universe would not be the same. Without gravity, the Earth would never have formed. In fact, there would be no planets at all! Without air resistance, airplanes could not take off. Without friction, bicycles and cars could not move. And without magnetism, Earth's surface would be burnt to a crisp. All in all, it's safe to say that these four forces help us a lot!

GRAVITY CAUSES THE MOON TO ORBIT AROUND THE EARTH.

Grounding Gravity

Gravity **attracts** all objects towards one another. Everything in the universe, including this book, has a gravitational pull that is trying to draw other objects towards it. The gravity made by the Earth is what keeps our feet firmly on the ground. Without gravity, we would simply float up into the sky.

YOU CAN'T FEEL THE GRAVITATIONAL PULL OF THIS BOOK BECAUSE IT IS TOO WEAK. THIS IS BECAUSE GRAVITY IS A VERY WEAK FORCE. FOR AN OBJECT TO HAVE A GRAVITATIONAL PULL THAT CAN ACTUALLY BE FELT, IT USUALLY NEEDS TO BE THE SIZE OF A PLANET.

GRAVITY PULLS US DOWN TO THE EARTH.

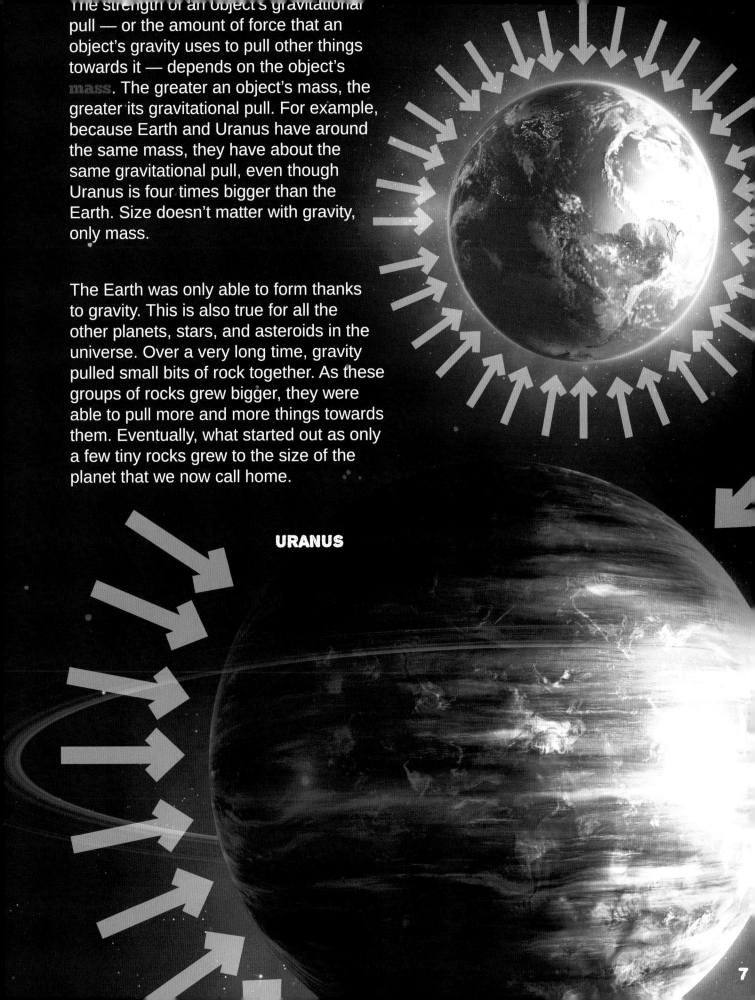

The strength of an object's gravitational pull — or the amount of force that an object's gravity uses to pull other things towards it — depends on the object's **mass**. The greater an object's mass, the greater its gravitational pull. For example, because Earth and Uranus have around the same mass, they have about the same gravitational pull, even though Uranus is four times bigger than the Earth. Size doesn't matter with gravity, only mass.

The Earth was only able to form thanks to gravity. This is also true for all the other planets, stars, and asteroids in the universe. Over a very long time, gravity pulled small bits of rock together. As these groups of rocks grew bigger, they were able to pull more and more things towards them. Eventually, what started out as only a few tiny rocks grew to the size of the planet that we now call home.

URANUS

Thrilling Falls

You may think that if objects with a lot of mass have a large gravitational pull, then they must fall faster than objects with less mass. However, this is not true. You can see this for yourself by trying the simple experiment below:

Step 1)

Find a ping-pong ball, a tennis ball, and a football. Notice how the ping-pong ball is the lightest and the football is the heaviest.

Step 2)

Drop all three balls at the same time and from the same height. You will notice that they all hit the ground at (roughly!) the same time.

The reason the balls all land at the same time is because gravity makes all objects **accelerate** at the same speed. It is true that the football has the greatest mass and so is being pulled by Earth's gravity with more force. However, because the football has more mass, it takes more force to get it moving. It doesn't matter how heavy something is — all things dropped near Earth's surface will fall at the same speed.

Air Resistance

Even though gravity pulls everything down at the same speed, you might notice that some objects fall more slowly than others. This is because of air resistance.

The air is made up of **gases**. Gases act in a similar way to liquids — objects can move through gases, but the faster the objects move, the harder it becomes. You can test this by moving your hands quickly underwater. It's hard to do! The water resists your hand. This is called water resistance. The same thing happens in the air, and is called air resistance, but the effect is much smaller.

Water resistance is much stronger than air resistance. This is because air has less mass than water. Because air has less mass, it is easier for falling objects to move it out of the way. Objects that are very good at moving air out of the way are described as **aerodynamic**. Aerodynamic objects, such as arrows, move very quickly through the air. Objects that are not aerodynamic, such as leaves and pieces of paper, fall slowly through the air. This is because air finds it difficult to get around these objects.

You can test the effect of air resistance yourself by dropping two sheets of paper. Crumple one up into a ball and leave the other flat. Drop them from the same height and at the same time. The crumpled ball will land first because it is more aerodynamic.

FLAT PAPER

CRUMPLED
PAPER

FLAT PAPER

Frightful Flight

Everything that flies uses air resistance to keep itself in the sky. Birds and airplanes use wings to resist the air and stay up! This works by changing the pressure of the air under the wings. Air pressure refers to how tightly packed together a patch of air is. The more something is squeezed together, the denser it becomes. This means it has less volume (takes up less space) but still has the same mass.

When high-pressure air — air that is tightly squeezed together — is released into low-pressure air, it quickly **expands**. This means that the air becomes the same volume and pressure as the air around it. Airplanes use this effect to fly.

When an airplane moves forward, air passes over and under its wings.

Due to the shape of an airplane's wings, the air is squeezed together when it moves underneath the wing. The high-pressure air pushes up against the wings of the airplane as it tries to expand into the low-pressure air above. This force from the high-pressure air is what pushes airplanes into the sky.

LOW-PRESSURE AIR

HIGH-PRESSURE AIR

Artificial Airplanes

The shape and size of an airplane's wings changes how well it can fly. You can see this for yourself — all you need is some paper. Check out the paper airplane designs on the next page and test how far they fly when you throw them. Afterwards, try out some of your own designs!

Before you start, you will need to draw out a table like the one below. When you throw an airplane, you are likely to do a few awkward throws. To get a fair result, you will need to throw each paper airplane four times, measure the distance of each throw, and record the best distance. Once you have all of your results, you can see which of the designs is best!

	TEST 1	TEST 2	TEST 3	TEST 4
AIRPLANE 1				
AIRPLANE 2				
AIRPLANE 3 (YOUR DESIGN)				

Design 1

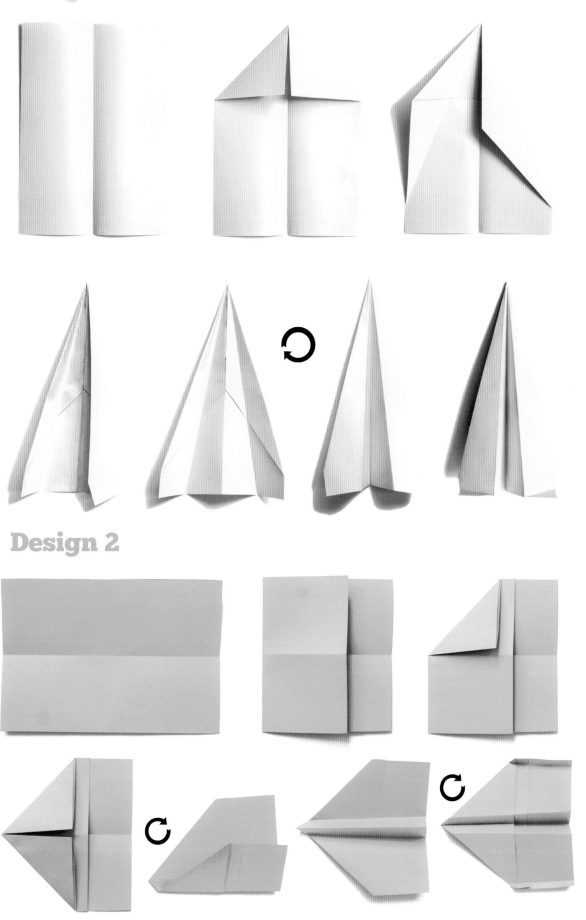

Design 2

Out-of-This-World Orbits

To orbit a planet means to move around it in a circular path. However, this doesn't mean that satellites orbiting the Earth are flying — in reality, they are constantly falling towards the Earth. The reason they do not crash down onto Earth's surface is because they are falling at an angle. But how does this work?

If you throw a ball straight into the air, it will come down in a straight line. However, if you throw a ball at an angle, its path through the air will curve as it comes back down.

If you could throw a ball hard enough at an angle, the curve of its fall would be so big that it would match the curve of the Earth. This would mean that the ground curved away from the ball as fast as the ball curved towards the ground. Because of this, the ball would never hit the ground. It would simply keep moving around the planet — unable to move away from the Earth due to gravity and unable to move towards the Earth due to its curved surface. Satellites work just like this.

Freaky Friction

Friction is a force that affects objects when they slide along against each other.

All objects are covered in bumps, dents, and tiny scratches. Even surfaces that appear very, very smooth have tiny **microscopic** bumps and dents on them. When two objects rub against each other, these bumps and dents knock together. As these bumps and dents knock together, it becomes harder for the two objects to slide past each other. This is friction. Surfaces that are very rough — or covered in many large bumps and dents — create more friction than surfaces that are very smooth.

Friction helps us to do everything from tying our shoes to riding a bike. Without friction, the tire of a bicycle would just spin on the spot.

This is because the friction grips the tire to the road. The rough surface of the bike's tire catches on the rough surface of the road, allowing the bike to move forward when you pedal. Friction also makes it so that you can stop. When you pull on the brakes, you stop the wheel from rolling and the tire drags along the road. This dragging causes friction between the tire and the road.

The force of friction changes when two surfaces are pressed together. The harder a surface is pressed against another surface, the harder it is to slide the surfaces against each other. You can try this yourself by pushing your hands together. When you push hard, it is more difficult to slide your hands against each other.

PEOPLE SKATE ON ICE BECAUSE IT IS VERY SMOOTH. THIS MEANS THAT IT DOESN'T CREATE A LOT OF FRICTION.

Fierce Friction

More friction is created when the surfaces sliding against each other are bigger. This is because more bumps and dents are knocking against each other. You can test this out with an easy experiment. All you need is two books.

Step 1)

Place the books on a table and open the first page of each book. Turn one book upside down so that you can place the first page of one book on top of the first page of the other book.

Step 2)

Overlap the pages of the two books, one by one. Keep doing this until all the pages of the books are linked together.

Warning: this could damage the books, so make sure that the books are old and no longer wanted.

Step 3)

Pick up the books and try to pull them apart. If the books you used have enough pages, the books will be impossible to pull apart!

The reason the books are so hard to pull apart is because each page is creating friction. If there were at least 200 pages overlapping each other, the force needed to pull the books apart should be the same as the force needed to drag a piece of paper that is 164 feet by 164 feet (50 m by 50 m) in size along the ground.

THIS SHEET OF PAPER WOULD BE ABOUT HALF THE SIZE OF A SOCCER FIELD.

Mighty Magnets

A magnet is a piece of metal that sticks to other metals — namely iron, nickel, and cobalt.

A magnet has two poles, or ends, known as the north pole and south pole.

Opposite poles on different magnets attract each other — the north pole on one magnet will be attracted towards the south pole on another magnet. The same poles on different magnets **repel** each other — south poles on different magnets will repel each other, as will north poles.

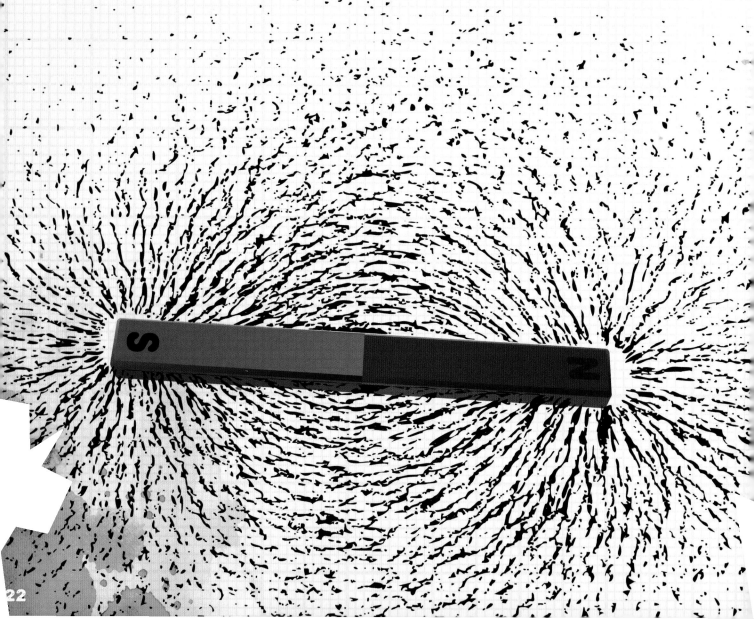

The poles on a magnet create a magnetic field around the magnet. Magnetic fields flow out of the north pole and back in the south pole. Magnetic fields can't be seen, but they do exist. When magnets are close together, their magnetic fields can interact and affect each other.

A small magnet with a weak magnetic force, like a fridge magnet, cannot affect other magnets unless they are very close together. Bigger magnets, on the other hand, can have much stronger magnetic fields and can affect things that are very far away. In fact, the Earth has its own magnetic field. Compasses use the Earth's magnetic field to tell us which way is north.

COMPASS

EARTH'S MAGNETIC FIELD

Compass
Confusion

For hundreds of years, compasses have helped humans to find their way home. The Earth's magnetic field makes the needle of a compass point north. However, it is possible to change the direction that a compass points.

To find out how magnetic forces affect compasses, you will need:

A COMPASS

Step 1)

Get your compass and hold it flat in your hand. The needle will point towards north. You can now adjust the base of the compass so the "North" mark lines up with the north-facing needle.

Step 2)

Point the positive end of your bar magnet towards the north of the compass. Then slowly drag the magnet around the edge of the compass and watch as the needle follows.

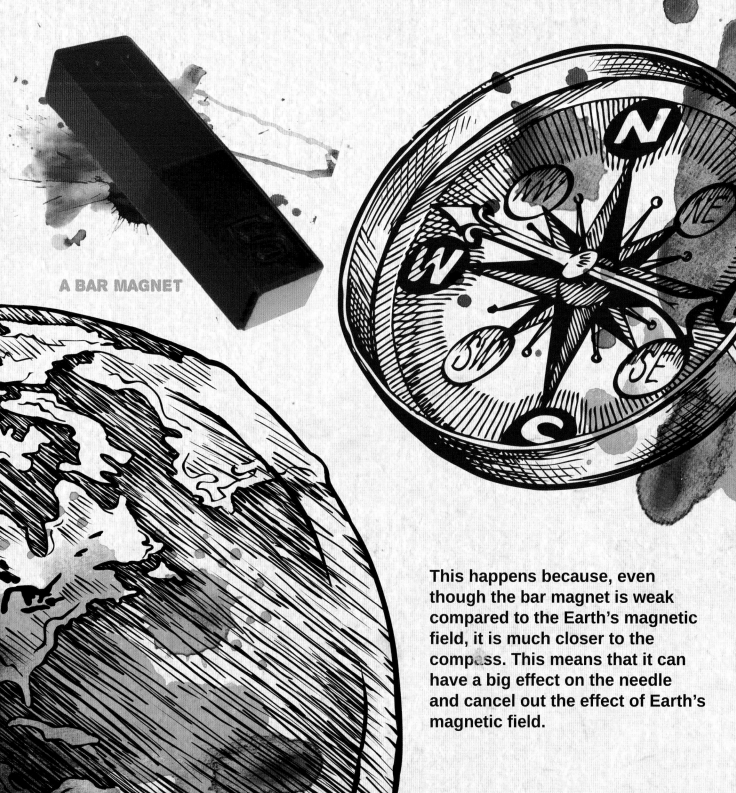

A BAR MAGNET

This happens because, even though the bar magnet is weak compared to the Earth's magnetic field, it is much closer to the compass. This means that it can have a big effect on the needle and cancel out the effect of Earth's magnetic field.

Strange Scientists

Sir Isaac Newton

Date of Birth: Jan 4, 1643

Date of Death: Mar 31, 1727

Place of Birth: England

Hobbies: Watching apples fall and figuring out the universe

Sir Isaac Newton was one of the most important **scientists** in human history. It was Newton who **discovered** how many of the forces in the universe work. One of the forces that Newton worked on was gravity. He is said to have thought of his **theory** of gravity while sitting under an apple tree. When an apple fell from the tree, he wondered why it fell in a straight line, rather than at an angle. After studying this, he figured out that everything is pulled towards the center of the Earth because this is where the Earth's mass is greatest.

Newton was also an **inventor**. He created the first working reflecting **telescope**. The telescope used a curved mirror to reflect light from space into a person's eyes. Light is used by our eyes to create a picture of the world around us. However, as the light from space is so dim, we need lots of it in order to see things in space in detail.

Reflecting telescopes use curved mirrors, which are far bigger than our eyes, in order to capture more light. The light is then directed into the person's eyes so that they can clearly see objects that are far away in space.

LIGHT

A NEWTONIAN TELESCOPE

Orville & Wilbur Wright

Date of Birth: Orville – Aug 19, 1871; Wilbur – Apr 16, 1867

Date of Death: Orville – Jan 30, 1948; Wilbur – May 30, 1912

Place of Birth: United States of America

Hobbies: Riding bicycles and building airplanes

150 years ago, reliable air travel didn't exist. Many people tried to create flying machines, but their inventions were problematic and often failed. Then, Orville and Wilbur Wright were born. These two brothers lived in the United States, where they built bicycles for a living. One day in 1899, however, they decided to put their bicycles aside and turn their attentions to the skies.

The Wright brothers started by building a wind tunnel. A wind tunnel is a large tunnel that you can blow smoke down. The smoke moves like air and can be seen. The Wright brothers used their wind tunnel to figure out how air flowed over the wing of a bird.

After many failed attempts to get their airplane off the ground, they finally did it in 1903. They managed to fly for a massive 12 seconds! Wait, what?

The length of the flight doesn't matter — this was the first airplane flight EVER! It must have seemed like magic at the time. Five years later, the Wright brothers had improved their method and had built a plane that could fly for over an hour. One hundred years later, people jump onto airplanes to fly all over the planet like it is the most normal thing in the world.

QUICK QUIZ

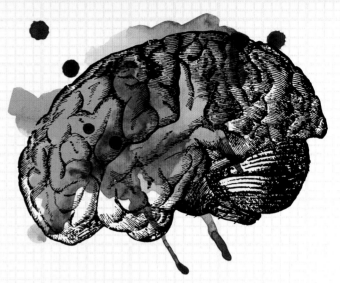

HAVE YOU TAKEN IT ALL IN? TAKE THIS QUICK QUIZ TO TEST YOUR KNOWLEDGE. THE ANSWERS ARE UPSIDE DOWN AT THE BOTTOM OF THE PAGE.

1. Which force pulls objects together?

2. What is the scientific word for weight?

3. If there was no air, everything would fall at the same speed. True or false?

4. What force keeps airplanes up in the air?

5. What do we call objects that orbit the Earth?

6. It is easier to stop a bicycle on a smooth surface than a rough surface. True or false?

7. What three metals do magnets stick to?

8. How many poles do magnets have?

9. What force is Sir Isaac Newton most famous for working on?

10. What vehicle did the Wright brothers invent?

1) Gravity 2) Mass 3) True 4) Air Resistance 5) Satellites 6) False 7) Iron, Nickel, and Cobalt 8) Two 9) Gravity 10) Airplane

GLOSSARY

accelerate	increase in speed
aerodynamic	a shape that reduces air resistance
asphalt	a material made from sand and gravel that is used to cover roads
attracts	pulls or draws towards
denser	more tightly packed
discovered	was the first to figure or work out
expands	becomes larger
gases	air-like substances that expand freely to fill any space available
interact	come together and affect each other
inventions	things, usually methods or devices, that have been created for the first time
inventor	a person who invents things as a job
mass	the amount of matter that an object contains
microscopic	so small it has to be viewed under a microscope
opposite	on the other side
planets	large bodies in space that move in orbits around stars
pressure	a continuous physical force on an object caused by something pressing against it
repel	push away
satellites	machines in space that travel around planets, take photographs, and collect and transmit information
scientists	a person who studies or has knowledge of science
telescope	a tool used to view distant objects
theory	a collection of ideas that are intended to explain something
universe	all existing matter and space considered as a whole

INDEX